These Birds Can't Fly

WITHDRAWN

By Allan Fowler

Consultants

Linda Cornwell, Learning Resource Consultant,
Indiana Department of Education

Janann V. Jenner, Ph.D.

Sharyn Fenwick, Elementary Science/Math Specialist
Gustavus Adolphus College, St. Peter, Minnesota

Children's Press®
A Division of Grolier Publishing
New York   London   Hong Kong   Sydney
Danbury, Connecticut

Visit Children's Press® on the Internet at:
http://publishing.grolier.com

Designer: Herman Adler Design Group
Photo Researcher: Caroline Anderson

Library of Congress Cataloging-in-Publication Data

Fowler, Allan.
    These birds can't fly / by Allan Fowler.
        p. cm. — (Rookie read-about science)
    Includes index.
        Summary: Briefly describes ostriches, emus, cassowaries, and kiwis—flightless
birds known as ratites—as well as another bird that cannot fly, the penguin.
        ISBN 0-516-20798-9 (lib. bdg.)   0-516-26420-6 (pbk)
        1. Ratites—Juvenile literature. [1. Ratites. 2. Penguins. 3. Birds.]
    I. Title. II. Series.
    QL676.2.F688   1998
    598.5—dc21   97-26722
                                                                 CIP
                                                                 AC

Did you ever wish you could fly like a bird?

Great egret

Bald eagle

Eagles can soar and
hummingbirds whiz about.
But not all birds can fly.

Ostriches and penguins have large bodies and small wings.

Their wings aren't strong
enough to lift such heavy
bodies off the ground.

Ostriches can run very fast
on their long, strong legs.
An ostrich can sprint faster
than a horse gallops.

Male ostriches are black and white, while females are brown.

Ostriches live in Africa
and are the largest birds
in the world.

Some males are 9 feet
tall and weigh more
than 300 pounds.

Females are not quite
that big.

People used to decorate hats with feathers from the tails and wings of male ostriches. Hunters who collected the feathers killed almost all the ostriches.

Today, ostriches are raised
on farms. Their skins are
used to make leather.

An ostrich's nest is a shallow hole in the middle of the grassy African plain. Ostriches can lay many eggs at the same time.

Each egg weighs about three pounds. That's as much as twenty chicken eggs.

Rheas are closely related to ostriches, but only half as tall.

They live in South America.

Emus are smaller than ostriches, but larger than rheas. They have rough brown feathers.

Emus live in Australia.
They call to each other
with loud yells.

Cassowaries live
in Australia, too.

A cassowary has shiny black
feathers that look like hair.
Look at that bright red
wattle on its neck!

Kiwis live in New Zealand.
They have short legs and are
no bigger than most chickens.

They hunt at night for berries, seeds, worms, and insects.

A penguin's legs are even
shorter than a kiwi's legs.

With their white breasts
and dark backs, they
look like men dressed
in evening clothes.

A penguin uses its wings
like a fish uses its fins—
to swim very fast.

On land, penguins waddle along on their webbed feet. When the ground is covered with snow, a penguin slides on its belly.

Penguins nest together
in huge groups
called colonies.

There may be as many
penguins in a colony
as there are people in
a big city.

Most penguins live in Antarctica. They eat fish and other sea animals.

It's true that you can't fly like a bird.

But you can run like an ostrich and swim like a penguin—only not as fast.

Words You Know

cassowary

eagle

emu

kiwi

ostrich

penguin

penguin colony

rhea

Index

Africa, 9, 12

Antarctica, 28

Australia, 17–18

cassowary, 18–19, 30

chickens, 13, 20

eagle, 4, 30

emu, 16–17, 30

coloring, 8, 16, 19, 23

feathers, 10, 16, 19

food, 21, 28

great egret, 3

horse, 7

hummingbird, 4

kiwi, 20–22, 30

legs, 20, 22

movement, 7, 25, 29

nest, 12, 26

New Zealand, 20

ostrich, 4–14, 16, 31

ostrich eggs, 12–13

ostrich farm, 11

ostrich skins, 11

penguin, 5–6, 22–28, 31

penguin colony, 26–27, 31

rhea, 14–16, 31

size, 9, 13–14, 16, 20

South America, 15

wattle, 19

wings, 6, 10, 24

About the Author

Allan Fowler is a freelance writer with a background in advertising. Born in New York, he lives in Chicago now and enjoys traveling.

Photo Credits

©: Ellis Nature Photography: 16, 22, 23, 26, 30 bottom left, 31 bottom left (Gerry Ellis), 3 (Walt Enders), 5, 30 top right (Terry Whittaker), cover, 15, 19, 25, 28 (Konrad Wothe); Photo Researchers: 5, 31 top left (Mark N. Boulton/National Audubon Society), 11 (Nigel Dennis), 7 (Clem Haagner), 8 (George Kleiman), 12 (Norman R. Lightfoot), 17, 20, 21, 30 bottom right (Tom McHugh); Tony Stone Images/Hulton Getty Picture Collection: 10; Visuals Unlimited: 14, 31 bottom right (W. Anderson), 13 (Bill Beatty), 18, 30 top left (John D. Cunningham), 6, 24, 31 top right (Kjell B. Sandved).